A Note to Parents and

Eyewitness Readers is a compelling new reading programme for children. *Eyewitness* has become the most trusted name in illustrated books, and this new series combines the highly visual *Eyewitness* approach with engaging, easy-to-read stories. Each *Eyewitness Reader* is guaranteed to capture a child's interest while developing his or her reading skills, general knowledge and love of reading.

The books are written by leading children's authors and are designed in conjunction with literacy experts, including Cliff Moon M.Ed., Honorary Fellow of the University of Reading. Cliff Moon spent many years as a teacher and teacher educator specializing in reading. He has written more than 140 books for children and teachers, and he reviews regularly for teachers' journals.

The four levels of *Eyewitness Readers* are aimed at different reading abilities, enabling you to choose the books that are exactly right for each child.

Level 1 – Beginning to read
Level 2 – Beginning to read alone
Level 3 – Reading alone
Level 4 – Proficient readers

The "normal" age at which a child begins to read can be anywhere from three to eight years old, so these levels are only general guidelines. No matter which level you select, you can be sure that you're helping children learn to read, then read to learn!

www.dk.com

Editor Dawn Sirett
Art Editor Jane Horne

Senior Editor Linda Esposito
Senior Art Editor Diane Thistlethwaite
Production Melanie Dowland
Picture Researcher Cynthia Frazer
Jacket Designer Piers Tilbury
Illustrator Gill Tomblin
Specially commissioned photography
Steve Gorton
Building Consultant David Jeffrie

Reading Consultant
Cliff Moon, M.Ed.

Published in Great Britain by
Dorling Kindersley Limited
9 Henrietta Street
London WC2E 8PS

2 4 6 8 10 9 7 5 3 1

Eyewitness Readers™ is a trademark of
Dorling Kindersley Limited, London.

A CIP catalogue record for this book is
available from the British Library.

ISBN 0-7513-6260-3

Colour reproduction by Colourscan, Singapore
Printed and bound in Belgium by Proost

The publisher would like to thank the following for
their kind permission to reproduce their photographs:
Key: a=above, c=centre, b=below, l=left, r=right, t=top

Mark Azavedo Photolibrary: 26; **Sylvia Cordaiy Photo Library Ltd:**
Humphrey Evans 20–21, 20 t; **Ecoscene:** Ian Harwood 6–7; **Pictor
International:** front cover background t, 4–5, 31 t; **Powerstock
Photolibrary/Zefa:** 12–13, 14–15; **Quadrant Picture Library:** 10–11,
16–17; **Telegraph Colour Library:** Gloria H. Chomica front cover
background b, Mark Mattock/Planet Earth 8–9; **Travel Ink:**
Leslie Garland 18–19, Tony Page 18 inset, 32 crb.

Additional credits: Jenifer Hourle, Peter Kindersley Junior and
Wilfrid Wood (for appearing in this book); Hampstead Garden
Centre, London (for forklift truck and plants); Paul Bricknell, Mike
Dunning and Richard Leeney (additional photography for DK);
Andrea Sadler (additional picture research).

EYEWITNESS READERS

BEGINNING **1** TO READ

Big Machines

Written by Karen Wallace

London • New York • Sydney • Delhi

BIG machines do BIG jobs.
They can knock down
an old factory.

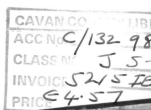

4

They can build a new park.
But how do big machines work?

A crane has a heavy ball.
The ball swings through the air.
CRASH!

It smashes into the factory wall!
Bricks and rubble
fall onto the ground.

rubble

SMASH!

CRASH!

SMASH!

A bulldozer has a huge blade.

SCRAPE!

SCRUNCH!
SCRAPE!

It pushes the rubble into a pile.
What will take
the pile of rubble away?

blade

A digger scoops up the rubble with a huge metal shovel.

The shovel dumps the rubble into a truck.

The truck takes the rubble away.

But where
is the truck?

shovel

Here comes the dumper truck!
The dumper has wide wheels
that can roll over bumpy ground.
It has high sides
so the rubble doesn't fall out.

wheel

13

The factory has gone.
It is time to build a pond
for the park.
An excavator (EX-kah-vay-ter)
digs a hole.
An excavator has a bucket
with metal teeth
that break up
the earth.

The bucket
dumps the earth
into a tipper truck.

But where
is that truck?

bucket

Here comes the tipper truck!
It is carrying new soil
for the park.

The back of the truck
goes up and
the tailgate opens.
WHOOSH! WHOOSH!

The soil slides
onto the ground.

WHOOSH!
WHOOSH!

tailgate

The pond needs concrete
to line its base.
A concrete mixer
brings concrete.
Its drum goes
round and round
and concrete pours out
of a special chute.

chute

When the concrete sets
it is hard and waterproof.

SERVICIO DE AGUA POTABLE 24 H.R.S.

The pond is finished but
now it needs water.
Here comes a water truck!

It has a big tank full of water
to fill up the pond.

The park needs a path
for people to walk on.

A roller has water
inside its wheels
to make the wheels heavy.

They press down on the path
until it is smooth and flat.

The park needs grass
for children to play on.
A forklift truck brings new turf.
Long forks lift up the turf and
carry it across
the park.

forks

The park needs plants.
A van brings trees and flowers.

Insects, animals and birds
will make the park their home.

The park needs a playground.
A big truck brings
swings and slides!
Big trucks carry things
all over the world.

Now the park is finished.

Children play on the grass.
People walk on the path.
Birds sing in the trees.
Can you remember
when the factory was there?

This man does.

BIG changes have happened.
Everything looks different.
BIG machines do BIG jobs!

Picture Word List

rubble

page 6

bucket

page 15

blade

page 8

tailgate

page 17

shovel

page 11

chute

page 18

wheel

page 13

forks

page 25